ELEGY OF A COMMON SOLDIER

AND OTHER POEMS

Dennis B Wilson

CONTENTS

CONTENTS

ELEGY OF A COMMON SOLDIER

The reflections of an ordinary soldier, of any
nationality, temporarily withdrawn from the front
line to an area of comparative peace, in any of the
wars to which unwilling Mankind has been
subjected by the ambitions, greed or stupidity of
his rulers.

Dennis B. Wilson

Elegy Of A Common Soldier

This is the Spring, and all around is seen
Nature awaking fresh, and giving birth
To eager buds and tender sheaves of green:
Spreading a growing cloak across the earth.
This is the time of youth and carefree love
Of which the minstrel sings, the poet dreams;
Of joyous sun, and peaceful skies above;
But this perfection is not all it seems:
For not too far across this pleasant world
The scene is changed: upon a sombre stage,
The sharpest weapons Man can forge are hurl'd
Against his fellow men, in bitter rage.
New life that seeks to pierce the desolation
Is churned by shell and bomb to reeking mud;
The season marked by God for fresh creation
Gives way to death: the green is tinged with blood.
No phrase is this from some medieval page;
No brutal sport in ignorance devised:
This is a learnéd scientific age:
An age of progress: Man is civilised ......

Civilisation .... was there ever heard
Such mockery in but a single word ?
For how sincerely can a nation claim
The rights of Man and progress as an aim,
Who then without a qualm resorts to force
To settle small disputes, which have their source
In sordid lust for pow'r and worldly gain ?
Man by grace of God possesses brain
Above the other creatures of the Earth;
Yet poorly he appreciates its worth.
Instead of guiding each inventive thought
On peaceful lines; and when he could have sought
To coax what pow'rs of nature he could find,
Improve his Earthly lot and aid Mankind;
He chose to work creating new machines
For hurling death by swifter, stronger means.
Empowered by God to use his fertile brain
For healing ills: alleviating pain:
He leaves the soothing balm, the saving knife,
To seek instead for ways of ending life.

Man wearied of restricting Earthly ties;
With yearning, gazed on free and boundless skies,
And could not rest content 'till he could own

The space where even birds had never flown.
To answer those with Luddite-minds, who cry
That only creatures born with wings should fly;
He promises to join in trade, as friends,
The peoples of the Earth's far distant ends.
And so the curse of war is now reveal'd
In regions far behind the battlefield,
Where simple homes and noble works of art
Are razed by sudden fire, or torn apart;
And women, children, agéd folk as well,
Are maimed and crushed beneath an air-borne hell
While Man, above the World on stolen wings,
His psalm of hate in exultation sings:
In bomb-enladen planes is swiftly hurl'd
To spread his 'bond of friendship' o'er the World.

When all the evil forces yield at last:
        The task is done:
The heart-ache and the anxious days are past,
        And vict'ry won:

If those we loved, who gave their lives to save
        A world insane,
Could leave awhile the silence of the grave:
        Could speak again:

They would not praise our valour, or the deed
        That won our day:
But list the things the living seldom heed,
        and this would say ....

"We are the dead of yet another war,
Our fathers died some twenty years before;
They also fought for all that we held dear,
To free Mankind from tyranny and fear;
And sacrificed the all they had to give
To win their sons the freeborn right to live:
        But we are dead....
        Why then are we dead ?"

"Yet must we watch the same mistakes unfold,
As age retires and yields its place to old:
While arms are built and shipped in mounting score

To bring our foes to battle-strength once more ?
We should be there to temper age with youth:
To counter false hypocrisy with truth.

But we are dead....
Why then are we dead ?"

"Though men will always publicly abhor
The anguish and futility of war,
They do not act until it is too late,
When peace has been consumed in fires of hate.
We would ensure our fight was not in vain:
That evil war should never rise again:
But we are dead....
Why then are we dead ?"

"Your victory has come, and well you fought,
But when the men who praise your deeds have done;
Then is the time to pause awhile in thought,
And ask yourselves the question, what was won ?"

"You sought for profit ? Then you sought in vain;
The mass of common people reap no gain.
Those statesmen who, by blundering mistakes
And lack of vision, cause these grim outbreaks
Of human conflict: they will still hold sway
In high, exulted posts, with handsome pay.
Your Service-chiefs will seize upon the chance
To practise favoured theories, and enhance
Those reputations scarcely earned before
In model battles: imitation war.
While men of commerce profit from their needs:
Supply them arms to consummate their deeds;
The very arms which, 'till the market's close
Were just as gladly sold to arm your foes.
And likewise profiteers will sell their hoards
For bloated sums no common wage affords,
(Though some there are, who weekly wages earn,
Who ever covet more, for less return).
These are the men who prosper day by day
While you, the hapless people, slowly pay
In taxes, sweat and blood, in futile strife;
In time, in health, in toil, in very life;
In lonely hearts that never cease to yearn
For those you love, who well may not return.
Yet politicians urge you on to more:
Crusading pleas and promises galore
'Till, when at last the bitter task is done,
The victory for which you fought is won,
You lie forgotten, 'mid your toil and pain,
'Till war demands your sacrifice again."

11

"You sought for glory ? There is none in war,
Among the truths historians ignore:
The tragic dust of battered town and home,
Reduced to wrecks which orphaned children roam;
The cold, unsheltered nights in dismal rain;
Exhausted men, who long for sleep in vain;
Confusion, noise and smoke, foul reeking mud,
And countless shattered bodies, oozing blood:
The pain before the final choking breath;
The vile decay, the sickly smell of death,
Which does not come triumphant or in rest
But suddenly, unheralded, or dress'd
In guise of hedgerow, tree or growing wheat,
Or lurks amid the flow'rs beneath your feet.
You seek the friend but lately by your side ?
Did you not hear ? He called you ere he died
And so escaped, thank God, a life of dread
Among the broken wrecks, the living dead;
The blind, the maimed and mentally deranged,
Condemned to live, from life itself estranged.
The battle lulls, to feed that secret fear
Of things unknown, but there are none to jeer,
For though each man is inwardly afraid,
Of hidden fear is courage truly made,
And for each hero by the World acclaimed
A countless number die alone, unnamed;
Forgotten by the ones they died to save,
To find cold glory in a foreign grave."

If those who pass would only pause and heed,
The fallen soldier's epitaph should read:

'The Youth who lies beneath this common earth
Could feel no hatred, no desire to kill;
Life's simple joys he loved at their true worth,
And only asked to live to take his fill.
The politics and causes that betray'd
His eager youth he did not understand,
But felt the ancient spirit of crusade
And sped to save his fresh-discovered Land.
And two such generations perished thus,
But those to come may yet escape their plight,
If ye who read complete the task for us
And win the peace, as we have won the fight."

Thus might our fallen sons address the world,
But they are dead, and all their counsel lost;

And not to us alone: in modern wars
The victor and the vanquished share the cost

    The experts court renown and fame;
    In warmth and comfort pledge their aim
    To list the crimes and fix the blame;
    And while their mighty brains devise,
    Another unknown soldier dies.

    For Mars, impatient God of War,
    Must all the time increase his score:
    A million lives ? A million more....
    A million weeping mothers, wives;
    A million empty, shattered lives.

    If all those experts, versed in laws
    From petty theft to monstrous wars,
    Set out instead to find the cause;
    Some good might then accrue from strife,
    And wholesale waste of human life.

    Impeach one nation, creed or man,
    But only human nature can
    Be blamed for wars since time began;
    Through selfish greed, through vanity,
    Through lack of real humanity.

Man is the lord of all created things,
That is his creed, his vain and frequent boast;
And creatures of the earth, the sea and air,
He uses as they serve his purpose most.
"I am the master," hear that blatant cry,
"You are my serfs, where'er I choose to reign;
I am the judge if you shall live or die,
For I alone can think: I have the brain."
Yet are those creatures brainless if they strike
When hunger calls, and instinct must obey;
But seldom kill for greed or sake of killing,
And never on their brother species prey ?
While Man, supreme in brain and human wisdom,
Fosters an urge for Earthly pow'r, and then
Builds up a tow'r of wealth beyond his needs,
Upon the ruined hopes of other men.
O senseless Man who, in thy selfish glory,
Blindly believe that you alone are wise,
Search for true wisdom: find the key to life

Among the very creatures you despise.

When God evolved the Universe
He made this planet small,
That none should feel too far remote
And each aware of all.
And yet he made it large enough
That all who pleasured there
Inherited the World's great gifts,
And each a worthy share.

And then he left the human race,
Without a cause for strife,
To seek its own salvation
And the hidden key to life:
Protected by His blessing,
With the best that He could give;
Secure from want and tyranny,
To love, and laugh and live.

But Man ignored this simple code of life
To conquer, first the animals, and then,
His lust for wealth and tyranny aroused,
To play the king and rule his fellow men;
To profit from the simple, trusting folk
Who only wish for peace to till the soil,
And live as God intended they should live:
To earn their daily food by useful toil.

The master's wealth increased; too soon there rose
His barriers of class, his useless snobs,
Who cast aside all fellowship with those
Who did the common, necessary jobs.

The well-fed rich in idle comfort sat,
To plan the varied pleasures of the day;
While others with an equal right to live,
In filthy slum must beg and scrape their way.

The despot built his armaments of war
And cruelly undermined his people's health:
He sacrificed religious faiths, to feed
His soul-destroying creed of pow'r and wealth.

The best of nature's gifts are free....
To those who can afford

To sacrifice their work in town
And seek that priceless hoard;
For nature's charms are rather shy,
And spurn the ways of Man:
Are driven by his ugly works
To prosper where they can.

Though Man may strive for freedom sweet,
He only wins the right
To live in thrall of life itself;
A bitter, endless fight
To keep beyond the stranglehold
Of waiting poverty;
For where the pow'r of money rules
The rich alone are free.

The World is fertile: ev'ry fruitful plain
May yield abundant crops of thriving grain;
Yet countless wasted acres ran to seed
'Till profits grew, as war increased the need;
And land that had been barren until now
Was forced to yield to unrelenting plough.
If all these plots, however large or small,
In wartime can produce enough for all,
Then why should this production ever cease
To yield sufficient food for all in peace ?
The fertile miles of grain and pastureland
Could puzzle future years to understand
Those evil days their hist'ry books supply,
When men could thirst and starve, and slowly die
From want of those necessities to live
Which nature waited patiently to give.

The earth is rich: above where food is grown;
With minerals beneath to depths unknown;
And yet, with all the wealth of nature there
For Man to find or cultivate, and share;
He has to work, and ere his toil is done,
He has to fight to keep what he has won;
Against his fellow men, consumed by greed,
For more than normal lives could ever need.

This was a lovely world that God had made:
The sun for light and warmth, and cooling shade
From trees in mighty forests, woodland bow'rs,
And friendly gardens, rich with fruit and flow'rs.
Warm, sheltered valleys quietly lay between

The graceful slopes of hills arrayed in green;
Or stately mountain-side, whose distant peak
Would hint of other lands for Man to seek.
And not in earth alone God sought to please,
But with the restless majesty of seas,
And patient calm of lakes and laughing streams,
He made a world surpassing mortal dreams.
How must He, since creation's birth, have grieved
To see the fate of all that He conceived:
The unassuming beauty of His plan:
Replaced by vast and ugly works of Man.
Great factories, their chimneys belching soot;
Mountains of slag, where pits have taken root;
Wide sprawling roads, and air-polluting trains;
Great throbbing towns, where shabby dullness reigns
In rows of shame-faced, uniform abodes
That, serpent-like, invade the country roads.
And Man, for these foul monuments, neglects
The clean and healthy world of God: rejects
His kingship over creatures great and small,
And proves himself the vilest of them all.

Two thousand years ago a man was born
Who loved the weak and sinful human race;
Who treated all hypocrisy with scorn,
And spread his blesséd wisdom without trace
Of condescension, prejudice or fear.
He spoke with equal zest to ev'ry creed,
To rich or poor, to all who came to hear;
For King or tramp alike He spread the seed
Of tolerance, equality and peace.
But those who, in the past, the crowd had sway'd,
Jealous to see their wealth and pow'r decrease,
A bribe of thirty silver pieces paid
For Jesus Christ, who only dwelt with men
To show them, by example, how to live:
His motive purely love. Who even then,
Before He died, in mercy could forgive
The people who, with inborn dread of law,
In doubt and fear stood silently aside
As, understanding not the things they saw,
They watched their own salvation crucified.

A faithful few there were of those who heard,
Though persecution often barred their way,
Who gave to future centuries the Word
Of true humanity. It lives today

While prelates seek, from pulpits far and near,
The boon of Christian fellowship to teach;
Yet few there are who live by what they hear,
And sadly few who practise what they preach.

The Prayer

Oh God, we are so weak of will,
So apt to think the worst of all;
So keen to render others ill,
Or hold our fellow men in thrall:
Selfish in our lives each day,
Seeking only pow'r and gain;
Jealous, and to envy prey,
Thoughtless, faithless, proud and vain.
In these and in so many ways
We differ from Thy holy plan
And yet, throughout our petty days,
Remain Thy nearest image, Man;
In whom all ills and faults are rife,
Yet lacks real evil in his heart;
Who yearns to live a truer life
But knows now how or where to start.

Forgive us our unworthiness, dear Lord,
And show us how to love and understand
Our fellow men, whose outlook we ignor'd,
Of other classes, creeds, or foreign land;
And help us, on this tolerance, to build
A finer life, of purpose, faith and zeal,
Until our guided striving has reveal'd
A World that shapes at last to Thy ideal.
So, when we come to You, not unafraid,
We may have cause to hope that we are worth
That other World for Man which Thou hast made,
And find the peace we so forsook on Earth.

Written at various times in 1943, 1944 and 1945; some parts written in slit-trenches in Normandy, making unauthorised use of the Field Service Pocket Book; and some parts written clumsily with the left hand while in hospital.

Armistice Day

The first maroons explode, a hush descends;
The crowd is silent, as the echoes cease.
They are asleep: on us alone depends
This yearly pray'r for blesséd, lasting peace.

Can we fail them, who rallied to the cause
Of freedom: dying for us in foreign lands ?
Though too young then, to join in bitter wars;
Our duty now lies written in the sands.

Not to forget the sacrifice they made,
But honour them until the final day:
With these two minutes remembrance must not face
And, like the last maroon, soon die away.

November 11th 1937 .....

Lesson of Life

One lesson all should learn from life, but often learn too late;
To make the most of what we have and sometimes under-rate.
The beautiful relationships: the happy hours we spend:
All laughter, and the joys of love, will one day reach an end.
Yearn not for what completed dreams the future may endow;
Brood not upon the might-have-been, enjoy the here-and-now.
Be grateful for the gift of hours that charm but cannot last,
Before the living present-time becomes the mourned-for past.
Allow no pride or unsolved hurt to spoil them in their prime,
For fear those few and precious hours should end before their time.
The sun may warm us through the day, but in the end it sets,
So build up happy memories instead of sad regrets.

..... 25th April 2012

The Little Lanes of England

(The first verse was a framed poem, seen
in a shop window in 1938, Author Unknown)

The little lanes of England,
That wind among the trees,
Spread out a net of memories
Across the seven seas;
They woo the exile's lonely heart
With thoughts of home again:
The little lanes of England
Have magic in their train.

'Mid forests tall, where ancient oaks
Their stately boughs extend;
O'er hills and dales, by cottage homes,
Those lanes of England wend.
The lonely exile's whole heart yearns
For England once again;
To walk through English country-side,
And roam each leafy lane.

Those friendly lanes, with bord'ring hedge
And banks of mossy green
Where flow'rs grow, wild and beautiful,
In gardens rarely seen.
The exile oft would sell his soul
To dwell there once again
In some neat thatch-roofed cottage,
Down an English country lane.

The little lanes of England,
That wind among the trees,
Spread out a net of memories
Across the seven seas;
They woo the exile's lonely heart
With thoughts of home again:
The little lanes of England
Have magic in their train.

September 1938

Word Failure

He gazed upon the scene; his heart was fired
With sudden realisation: felt inspired
To write of all the beauty that he knew;
Of fleecy clouds that race across the blue;
Of sunshine after cooling Summer show'rs,
And rainbow's varied hues that matched the flow'rs;
Of sailing ships that glide o'er crested seas,
And leaves of Autumn, falling with the breeze;
Of sunsets, and the sky with gold aglow;
Or trees and meadows, white with Winter snow.
Of daffodils, awaking in the Spring,
And cottage walls, where Summer roses cling;
Of forest glade, and ancient oak serene
By slowly winding paths of mossy green;
Of fields of golden wheat: of placid lake:
Of sandy shores where sea-waves gently break.
The hush as ev'ning shadows softly fall,
Or morning sun's first rays upon the wall:
Of lightning flash across a stormy sky.
Of these he thought to write yet, with a sigh,
He threw away his pen; for who was he
To write of beauty, there for all to see ?

15th October 1939

Closing Account

The lifteime that we spend on care-bound Earth
Is one of struggle, seeking cause or aim;
Each striving for the thing he holds most worth;
It may be peace, or wealth, or pow'r or fame.

But death makes beggars out of Earthly kings,
No matter how much pow'r each hath possess'd:
Who sees futility in worldly things
Alone deserves Eternal peace and rest.

Then, just as at the closing of a day,
And softly as the twilight shadows creep,
The hand of Death will halt our Earthly way
And quietly lead us into blissful sleep.

So gently; as a slowly flowing stream
The moss-grown banks of woodland doth caress,
There comes at last this sleep which bears no dream:
A sleep which brings us sweet forgetfulness.

May 5th 1940

Ships That Pass

The great swift liner steamed her way
Across the ocean wide;
Two thousand passengers enjoyed
The luxury inside:
A palace, glittering and gilt;
Exquisite carvings, finest art
Adorned the walls, of priceless worth:
Of such is formed a liner's heart.
But presently she overtook
A dirty tramp and small,
So rusty were her plates she seemed
To bear no paint at all.
The passengers scarce deigned to look,
And those who did, just sneered
Or joked in ignorant contempt,
"A filthy tub," they jeered.
The tramp just plodded slowly on
Across the wavecrests white;
The liner glided switly by
And soon was lost to sight.

The months passed by, reports of war
Monopolized the news;
The great ship now lay harbour-bound,
Too beautiful to use:
But in another berth, the tramp
Prepared to sail once more;
The months had left her dirtier still,
More rusty than before:
But guns were mounted fore and aft,
And battered plates, although
Slight damage, proudly spoke
Of combat with the foe:
Of service in her country's name
In mine-infested seas,
For English folk at home depend
For food, on ships like these.
The liner silent lay, to rust
From inactivity;
The lowly tramp, a job to do,
Steamed proudly out to sea.

May 8th 1940

Although the above was true at the time the poem was written, it did not remain so for long. The "Queen Mary" and "Queen Elizabeth," (the latter never having been in service previously), were converted into troopships and gave tremendous service throughout the war. The "Normandie" was laid up in New York harbour at the outset of the war and until taken over by the United States in 1942, but just before her first voyage under the American flag she was completely gutted by fire, and was eventually broken up.

When Daphne Dances

Fair Daphne is, when dancing,
Sweetest smile upon her face,
Supremest peak of loveliness:
Epitome of grace.

No leaf which falls on mossy turf,
Where April primrose hides,
Could lighter touch the ground than she,
So daintily she glides.

The sunny smile that dwells within
Her eyes, so starry-pearl'd;
As Daphne dances, drives away
The cares of all the World.

Should all the stars extinguished be,
T'would not the ev'ning mar;
For Daphne, when she dances,
Can outshine the brightest star.

10th May 1940

The Land Beyond

There lies, beyond the snow-capped peaks,
A land surpassing fair
Where weary, suffocated souls
Can breathe fresh, scented air:
A land which brings to noise-wracked nerves
A peace, which heals and mends;
Beyond the far horizon,
Where the soft-hued rainbow ends.

Away beyond the fleecy clouds
That race across the sky,
There lies this land of sweet heart-ease,
To greet us when we die:
No need to strive for wealth or pow'r.
As in our Earthly lives
For, in this lovely land beyond,
The Christian spirit thrives.

A spacious garden, rich with trees
And softly flowing streams;
A land so lovely, no one need
Indulge in futile dreams,
But rest in quiet beneath the shade
When daily toil is done:
Beyond the farthest chartered stars;
Beyond the moon and sun.

23rd may 1940

Bruerne

In changing seasons through the years,
In weather wet and dry,
This stately house, for countless days,
Has smiled on passers-by;
Has lent cool shade in Summertime
To cricket on the lawn;
Seen many a night sky sunset-hued:
Slept quiet 'till the rosy dawn;
Has known the joy of Christmastide,
As snowflakes softly fall:
Excited hush of Christmas Eve,
With carols in the hall.
The echoes, that have filled this house
From cellar up to rafter,
Have told of sickness, lean times, health,
Of sadness, wealth and laughter.
The stories, could these walls but speak,
Would fill an endless page
Of how this house, in peace and war,
Grew statelier with age.

But now, alas ! This grand old house,
Of furnishings bereft,
Is like a festive banquet-hall,
When all the guests have left.
The echoes, now so few and rare,
A hollow note contain:
They cry aloud for company,
A puzzled, hurt refrain.
For fate condemns this lovely house,
That many grew to bless,
To stand, with bleak and lonely face,
In silent emptiness.

21st June 1940.

"Bruerne" was the Nursing Home in Southsea run by my Aunt, Isabella Marie Wilson, where I spent many holidays and traditional Christmasses which, when my father was on leave from India, were the only periods when he and my Mother, and my brother Adrian, my sister Daphne and I were together as a family, (for reasons explained in my father's biography "The Secret Lives of a Secret Agent" by Tim Crook, Kultura Press). In June 1940 my aunt moved what had by then become a retirement home for the elderly to "Mount Howe," Topsham, South Devon. "Bruerne" was demolished in the year of my Aunt's death in 1959, the work commencing on the actual day of her funeral in Southsea.

Topsham

From happy little Topsham,
Where the Exe flows out to sea,
I hear a soft, insistent voice
That ever calls to me.
Perhaps the surging wavelets
Have a message to impart;
Or is the lovely countryside
Still tugging at my heart?
Perhaps the village lures me,
With its houses, quaint to see;
Or do the tree-clad hills beyond
Keep beckoning to me ?
It may be sprites have bound me
In a strong enchanted spell;
Perhaps the Devon pixie-folk,
Perhaps: I cannot tell.
I know that if I had my choice
It's there I'd wish to be;
In peaceful little Topsham,
Where the Exe flows out to sea.

19th August 1940

Resurrection

An oak tree in a meadow stood,
Fresh green its leaves, and young its wood:
The acorns, born in Summer days,
Found life within the blesséd rays
Of sun for, as an oak tree thrives,
It nurtures countless future lives.
But soon an Autumn sun shone down
On withered leaves of russet brown
Which bore, amid their tints of gold,
The loveliness of all things old.
A wind sped fast upon the air,
Which stripped the oak and left it bare;
The acorns fell upon the earth:
The mother tree had given birth.
The weary leaves a rest place found,
And nestled close against the ground
And, with the aid of Winter rain,
Enriched the precious soil again
Which fed, in turn the oak tree's roots.
Then, in the Spring, the tender shoots
Burst forth again in green young leaves
And acorns in their cup-like sleeves,
Breathing the air, so fresh and sweet:
And Nature's cycle grew complete.

The oak tree lived a lengthy age,
Braving the might of Nature's rage;
The bitter cold, the Wind's cruel lash,
The tempest's roar, the lightning flash;
Until the weary heart inside
Became too tired to live, and died.
And yet within that death it found
New life, in all the trees around;
For where the oak alone had stood
There thrived a large and spreading wood,
And in each oak flowed, young and free,
The life-blood of the mother tree.
So Nature deals with all of us
And grants us endless life: and thus
We fall in time, and sleeping lie,
Yet never altogether die;
But leave this scene of noise and strife
And find, in death, another life.

16th October 1940

Mount Howe
(Topsham, South Devon)

Here there is music; where, through each fleeting day,
A wingéd chorus, high in the rustling trees,
Sings of a world that's beautiful and gay;
Enriching the air with lovely melodies.
The trees join in, and sigh with sheer content,
Swayed by the wind; and coloured butterflies,
That dance between the flow'rs in merriment,
Linger with faint and soothing lullabies
From beating wings. Thus breathes the fragrant air
A sweet refrain, that hardly seems to cease;
Bringing the heart-ease only peace can bear,
Here where the world is quiet, for here lies peace.

Here there is beauty, here, where a scene unfolds,
Causing the heart in wonderment to still,
Of trees and fields in mingled greens and golds,
And toy-like hamlet, on the distant hill.
Bordered by trees, a river slowly wends,
While kindly sun bestows a smiling glance;
And where, by reflected trees, the river bends,
The clearly mirrored sunbeams play and dance.
The stately trees, that shield the sun's bright glare,
And sway in answer to the wind's caress,
Look up to Heaven and breathe a silent pray'r,
Softly to God, for all this loveliness.

20th October 1940

Peace of Mind

One magic night, I strode beside
The Exe, as still it lay,
As though the waves were resting
From their labours through the day.
Upon it shone the splendour
Of the moon, that rode so high,
And spread a gentle radiance
Across the lifeless sky.

The moon upon the water
Such a tragic aspect had;
So incalculably lonely,
And so infinitely sad;
That the worries and the cares,
Which had seemed so great to me,
Were as nothing when compared
To the sadness of the sea.

So I threw them all away
Past the waters, moonbeam kiss'd,
And beyond the toy-like sailing boats
They vanished in the mist.
And my weary soul was cleansed
Of the cares that chafe and vex;
And my troubled heart lay still
As the moonlight, on the Exe.

November 1st 1940

Impossible Dreams

The Providence that rules our lives
Intends to make quite clear
The gulf, between the World Beyond,
And all we know of here;
So firmly sees that none of us
Who on this Earth reside,
Regardless of his wealth or state,
Is ever satisfied.
Thus each must nurse, it matters not
What wealth or pow'r he gain,
A secret wish within his heart,
For which he yearns in vain.
And ev'ryone has this; a shrine
To worship from afar:
The hopeless, aching longing
Of the mortal for a star.
And this must be our lot on Earth,
Since Fate ordains that each
Shall vainly dream and yearn for that
Which lies beyond his reach.
But Fate is never all unkind,
And sees that hope is there;
To sow in Man the will to live,
And lighten his despair:
The hope that in a sweeter World,
Away from Earthly strife,
He may receive that vain desire;
The dream that filled his life.

9th November 1940

Separation

Few of life's occasions
Can, than parting, bring more pain;
When all that we have loved is past,
And life must start again;
When the question keeps recurring
With an extra stab of pain
Through the lonely, aching heartbreak,
"Will we ever meet again ?"
And ugly doubts that haunt the mind,
Each thought and dream to fill,
Of, "Will you always be the same ?"
And, "Will you love me still ?"
But doubts must stay unanswered
And the pain feel no relief,
While all the happy memories
Dissolve in hopeless grief.
And though this parting anguish
Day by day grows slowly less,
For only time can fully heal
The soul's deep loneliness;
Until all doubts are answered
As the future makes reply,
Ev'ry parting must be tragic:
Hearts must break at each, "Goodbye."

21st December 1940

Bereft

Now that you are gone, and I must bear
The penetrating ache of loneliness
That fills my heart, alone; for who can share
Or even help to ease, my soul's distress;
When ev'ry waking thought and ev'ry dream
Recalls your radiant loveliness again:
When all you are, and all your actions seem
So vividly remembered in my brain ?
The music of your voice; that lovely smile
Which, in a care-wracked world, changed tears to mirth,
And brightened up its dullness for a while:
These fragments linger still. Stray thoughts give birth
To memories which I am loath to kill,
And oft on purpose summon back again,
Although this all-of-you that I have still
Can bring no change of heart, save deeper pain.

2nd January 1941

Arts In Conflict

An artist and a poet stood
Upon a hill, and saw
A scene of lovely countryside,
Which filled them both with awe.
The artist set his easel up
Upon the hilltop green,
And set to work, with brush and paint,
To reproduce the scene.
The poet scarcely seemed to care:
Apparently he lazed;
Yet all the time his mind worked hard
As on the scene he gazed.
The artist, in a while, remarked,
"Though different in name,
Our trades are closely interlocked:
Our work is much the same.
For I paint scenes with brush and paint;
You paint in words and rhymes ...."
The poet broke in, "Not so, friend,
I'll not compound your crimes !
May Nature never pardon you
The loveliness you taint,
By setting it on canvasses
With smears of oily paint.
In words a poet may paint scenes
Like you, but as a whole
He writes of things as they appear
Reflected by his Soul.
Thus poetry, in ev'ry sense,
Is pure, ethereal art;
Inspired by realisation,
And emotion, and the heart."

2nd February 1941

Disconsolation

When those we love have gone away:
Their happy laughter heard no more;
As though a portion of ourselves
Lies hidden by a bolted door;
No kindly word, no cheerful thought
Can bring the lonely soul relief:
No hope of future pleasure lift
The ever-present weight of grief.
All former never-failing joys
Quite empty seem, and comfortless;
While memories of happy hours
Will dwindle then to nothingness,
Beside the bitter tragedy
That even simple things assume:
A song we once together sang;
A vacant chair; an empty room.

5th February 1941

A Sunset Over Topsham

All day this once-so-pleasing scene,
With seeming endless rain between,
Was marred by gloom, and sombre clouds
That dressed the hills in mourning shrouds;
While sullen waves must needs defile
The river's normal tranquil smile.
Then suddenly, as though to pay
For care and sorrows through the day,
The down-pour ceased and sunset came
To pierce the clouds with points of flame.
And now the river seems to flow
With molten fire; and all the glow,
As though with some magician's wand,
Transforms the fields and hills beyond
And drapes them all in cloaks of red.
Then these reflections grow and spread
'Till all that has been touched by rain,
The trees and flowers, all attain
The varied tints of reds and golds
That highly burnished copper holds.
And now the whole world seems afire:
To form a massive, joyful pyre
Of gloom and cares that marked the day.
But as these realms of colours gay
The highest peaks of splendour climb,
They pause, for but a fleeting time
Then, since all Earthly glories end,
Commence to fade and softly blend
With sullen clouds and azure sky.
The flames burn low, then slowly die:
The gorgeous reds and purples shrink
To fragile mauve and coral pink,
Which linger in the stormy West
Where good King Sol now lies at rest.

12th February 1941

The Balm Of Water

All ye with hearts that are wearied and torn
By the fight for existence, and by trouble worn;
Seek thou a road that goes wandering wide
Through the wealth that is England's: her fair countryside;
Where a waterfall murmurs and cool streams abound,
And feel those cares lighten and flee with the sound
Of running water.

Is there a remedy surer, for care,
Than sweet running water, in fact, anywhere ?
Water that follows an age-worn course,
Bordered by meadowland, forest and gorse;
Freely, contendedly winding along:
Mirth is the keynote, and carefree the song
Of running water.

Many a wanderer, weary indeed
Of a world that has wealth for its aim and a creed,
Rating Christian charity lower than gold,
Has discovered fresh hope; seen a new life unfold;
In a stream that is laughing its way to the sea
With the lighthearted music, untrammelled and free,
Of running water.

15th April 1941

Priceless Heritage

England: who would not fight for thee,
Who hath thy peerless beauties seen;
And gazed in silent wonderment
Upon thy vistas green;
Or walked beneath some ancient shade
Where patient oak trees stand,
And known that peace he cannot find
In any other Land ?
That glorious English countryside .....
Where sleepy hamlets lie
Unmarred by grim, progressive Time:
Can anyone deny
That here have sturdy Englishmen
The soul of freedom sown;
That here in fertile English soil
The roots of peace are grown ?

I thank the Providence that gave
Me birthright to that peace;
And to defend that freedom
That it may not fade, or cease
To bless the scattered loveliness
Within thy guardian bounds of sea:
Who would not gladly give his all,
England: who would not die for thee ?

21st August 1941

Reason and Faith

Can death end all: can all the lovely things
That bless this life, and opposites no less,
Be there without an aim; and all our lives,
Save for rewards for which a whole world strives,
Completely purposeless ?

Must all we know, and ev'rything we see,
Vanish at last in grim infinity;
As though Death snaps his fingers, and thereafter
Feeling and music, love and joyous laughter,
Abruptly cause to be ?

The Soul that bids us seek where beauty lies:
Inspires emotion, helps us realize
Each day some deeper love of lovely things,
And wonderment that understanding brings:
Surely that never dies ?

These things just cannot be; and in believing
The after-death is not eternal shade;
I find a peace that is beyond conceiving,
And death shall find me sad, but unafraid.

22nd October 1941

A Prayer

Grant, O Lord, that I each day
May better realize
The loveliness, that lies before
My unobservant eyes;
In things that seem beyond all hope;
In places grim and bare,
Where Thy redeeming Hand hath left
Some spark of beauty there.

Thenceforward, help me understand
The world which Thou has made;
And feel, and know, what lies beyond:
And grant me then Thine aid,
To phrase in verse the ecstasy
That understanding wrought:
Emotions far beyond mere words,
And scarce expressed in thought.

12th January 1942

Dead To Life

The man who feels no sudden urge to sing
When sunshine wakes the daffodils in Spring;
Or, when some gentle music fills the air,
Can sound his heart and find no echo there:
Who sees the shining universe at night
And is not thrilled to wonder at the sight;
Or gazes, thankless, on some stately tree;
Or watched the mighty rolling of the sea,
And felt no restless, thrilling urge to roam
Across its racing miles of crested foam:
To whom the simple joys of ev'ry day;
The happy cries of children as they play,
And all the priceless gems of Beauty's store
Are merely passing fancies, nothing more.

That man, who earns no love or kindly thought,
Or sympathy for ills that care has wrought,
Is fit indeed for any kind of sin
Because he has no living soul within.
Far better for the world if he had died
Than live, and be completely dead inside.

27th January 1942

Jean

Roaming this oft enchanting world,
Where beauty lives for those who seek
Humility, when lovely things
Defy the words that humans speak;
I treasure ev'ry vision rare,
And laughing eyes and auburn hair.

Hair that reflects the smiling light
Of sunbeams, 'neath each lock conceal'd;
Softly in waves across the brow,
Seeming a vain attempt to shield
That demon mischief lurking there
In laughing eyes, 'neath auburn hair.

Man by nature has to yearn
For treasures, his in dreams alone;
And yet in dreams aware of some
He dare not even hope to own.
Happy the man to even share
Those laughing eyes, and auburn hair.

30th May 1942

Sea Calling

Pity I have for any man
Who plans the sea as his career,
Against the wishes of his clan,
And then, perhaps in doubt or fear,
Draws back, although his soul was bent
To serve that yearned-for element.

Never to brave a tempest's roar
That Hell and angry nature wrought:
To watch each foaming mountain soar
As though a greedy Neptune sought,
Not satisfied with just a slave,
To drag him to an ocean grave.

Never to ride on crested wings
Above a snowy—fleckled sea,
When ev'ry fibre laughs and sings
The joy of being alive and free:
To watch the crested horses play,
And see the rainbows in the spray.

Or know by night the magic lull
When skies are clear; the sea a lake,
Saving around the vessel's hull
Where ripples gently stir and break;
And mirrored there in bright reverse
The wonders of the Universe.

O, I am old, and time has flown,
And dimmed my reminiscent store;
And all these things I joyed to own
Will come my lonely way no more;
Unless some other life may free
My soul, to roam the urgent sea.

June 1942

Scotland

Away up North beyond the Tweed,
You'll find a rather diff'rent breed
Of gentle-folk; to welcome slow
You'll think at first, but soon you know
Their friendly hearts. And then you find
They're witty, generous and kind:
Eager to give to those who need:
Thrifty, but never mean with greed;
And never mean of mind.

You'll like the change in countryside.
The tranquil lochs in shyness hide
Reflecting waters, deep and still;
To rouse a sudden breathless thrill
In weary folk who climb to seek
A view of them; and from the peak
Of noble mountain, purple brown,
To gaze in awe-struck silence down
As laughing streamlets hurry by,
Through vales where cosy farmsteads lie,
Unmarred by noise of town.

The English countryside is green,
The loveliest I've ever seen;
But should some unforeseen mishap
Erase fair England from the map;
Then would I gladly soothe my ills
Mid Scotland's warm and friendly hills;
Happy to live: content to lie
Amid the heather, sweet and dry,
Beneath those friendly hills.

April 15th 1944

To Ann

(Written for Capt. John Frary)

Since God evolved the world, and time began,
The centuries of life until this day
Record the long, eternal search of Man
To find a mate, ideal in ev'ry way.
I warrant but a precious few indeed
Completely find such ideal love; yet I,
Without a claim on Providence, succeed
Beyond my fondest dreams, when first I try.

Her hair is auburn: hidden lights of gold
Rival the smiling sun on Summer days;
Her eyes great depths of understanding hold:
But I for all eternity could gaze
On her perfection. Though I know not why
My God should make me such an envied man;
My heart will grateful be until I die
To Him who, of his mercy, gave me Ann.

22nd April 1944

To A Girl In A Railway Station

(Micheldever: Hampshire)

So proud her graceful bearing,
So confident her stride;
I verily would give my all
To saunter by her side:
From whence she comes, or whither rides,
These things I do not know;
But would that I could go with her,
That I might tell her so.

Thus Providence may, now and then,
Bedeck this Earthly plot
With such a glimpse of Paradise,
To charm our weary lot:
But stay ! There comes this bitter thought
To pierce me like a knife:
Some grunting train will rumble by
And take her from my life !

30th May 1944

Hurst Leigh

Some buildings live in human hearts
Through loveliness or ancient fame,
And neither of these attributes
Could you in honest phrases claim:
Your rooms were cheerless, cold and dim:
Your face foreboding, grey and grim.

And yet those dismal, draughty rooms
Had often echoed carefree mirth;
Your walls protected those within:
Through many storms had proved their worth;
And who could mock each rotting stair,
By countless schooboys trodden bare ?

Those schoolboys: some grown rich, some poor,
And some in fame and glory bask;
While many earn a meagre wage
Upon some dull, essential task.
So many varied paths they tread:
So many, lost in war, are dead.

And all their varied characters ,
Their very lives, in you were made;
But you are gone, and in your death
Their memories begin to fade;
And so my ageing heart dismays
To lose a link with early days.

4th June 1944

*Hurst Leigh School in Southampton was the small private school of
good past reputation, that I attended from 1929 to 1932, (because it was still
socially acceptable but cheap), by which time the old grim building that
housed it, like the education provided therein, had greatly deteriorated.
However I received a thorough grounding in English Grammar and Syntax,
and I was well educated in the subjects that meant most to me; English
literature and poetry, and English history. The building was demolished in
1944 and a block of flats erected.*

Ballerina

I watched a golden Autumn leaf
Rejoice in freedom found;
It spun upon a playful wind,
And lightly kissed the ground:
I saw this joyful thing
Although it was the Spring.

I also saw a pure-white swan,
That swam with queenly grace
Across a placid, shining lake,
And left a rippled trace:
I saw this, yet I swear
There was no water there.

I saw the hope of distant hills,
The sun in raiment bright;
The mischief of a laughing stream;
The magic of the night:
But I can give no proof,
With o'er my head a roof.

And though my view was bounded in
By four walls, gaunt and bare;
I gazed upon the World beyond
And found it bright and fair,
And sweet; and so entrancing;
For Margaret was dancing.

Margaret ("Midgy") Worlledge, who danced with the Anglo Polish Ballet.

15th March 1945

To The Nursing Services

Short while ago he dwelt with death,
'Mid battle's grisly pall;
No more a hero than the rest:
Or were they heroes, all ?
And now his mind could not escape
The ghastly things he'd seen;
The many former-stifled fears:
The awful might-have-been.

But soon those troubled thoughts were eased
By smiling girls in white,
Who gave him courage through the day
And helped him rest at night:
Who dressed his wounds with tender care
And minimum of pain;
Who gladly brought his ev'ry need,
And gave him faith again.

No fame or rich reward for them;
No pleasant, healthy task;
No glamour of the Services
In which their sisters bask:
Their lot to care for shattered men
'Till life and hope returns:
To work long hours and patiently,
And prove the lamp still burns.

18th March 1945

The Beauty Of Trees

If I, with palette, brush and paint,
The cultured world could please;
I'd spend my ev'ry working day
Recording lovely trees.
The pine, the beech, the grand old oak
That braves a thousand storms;
And sentinels of peace, arrayed
In silver uniforms:
The ash, the chestnut, elm and larch;
The willow, quiet and sad;
And brethren of the orchard
In their cheerful blossoms clad.

A tree is always lovely
Through the seasons of the year;
In Spring, when nature wakes the buds
And sudden leaves appear:
In Summer garb, when splendour reigns
In ev'ry forest glade;
And Autumn, with its patient calm
Before those glories fade;
For though you search throughout the world
No lovelier scene you'll find
Than trees, in golden Autumn,
With a setting sun behind.
And then, when bare, each limb reveals
The grace which thrills the sight
When cloaked in Winter's gleaming snow:
A tracery of white.

If thus I laboured all my years,
My task had scarce begun,
Before I laid aside my tools:
My thread of life was spun.
I think of all God's gifts to Man
He loved the tree the best;
So lay me in some woodland glade
And leave me there, to rest.

3rd April 1945

Reflections On Water

Musing, where a river
Through a grateful meadow ran,
I thought of how a flowing stream
Reflects the moods of Man:
Cheerful on the sunny days,
Bright when skies are clear;
Sullen when the clouds are grey,
Dull when storms appear;
Selfish in its flood of pow'r:
Proudly holding sway;
Heedless of the lesser streams
That feed it day by day;
Restless in its ordered path,
Yearning to be free;
Keen to breach its guiding banks
And swifter reach the sea;
Angry when obstructions rise,
Too bulky to ignore;
Merciless to any prey
That can resist no more;
Peaceful when its pow'r is spent,
Pausing then to pray;
Patient in the twilight hour:
Calm at close of day.
T'was thus I thought beside that stream:
Like molten silver, now;
Not harshly though, for Man compares
To far worse things, I vow.

8th April 1945

Victory Poems I and II

On April 18th 1945, when it was obvious that the war in Europe was coming to an end, the Daily Mail announced a competition for the best original poem to express the Nation's feelings in the hour of victory. More than 8000 readers submitted poems within the allotted ten days. At that time I was attached to the 30th Battalion of the Loyal Regiment, stationed in Penrith, Cumberland, where I was friendly with Stan Rumble of the Canadian Army, who was also attached to the Battalion. It was Stan for whom I wrote the poem "Audrey" on 10th May 1945, so that he could give it to his wife. He persuaded me that I should enter the contest, although I doubted if I could write a poem to order. In the event I wrote and entered two poems but, although they may have been in keeping with the general euphoria of that time, I knew that they did not express my own feelings, which were too mixed to put into verse. I felt that although it was right to feel relief and be glad that the evil forces had been defeated and the killing ended, it was wrong to rejoice in a victory that had cost so many lives and left so many bereaved. My two poems were rubbish really, and I do not think Stan was impressed either, and I was ashamed that I had submitted them when I read some of the poems published by the Daily Mail. The contest was won by G. I. Lee, who was a Private in the ATS, winning the first prize of £100, which was an appreciable amount in those days. As Archimedes discovered so dramatically, inspiration does not always come at the most convenient time, and it was not until 15th February 1947, when I wrote "Aftermath," that I was able to write my own true feelings about the war, in the only non-rhyming poem I have ever written. It might have been acceptable at that time, because by then we had all sobered up and faced the reality of what the war had meant in terms of human suffering, and the knowledge that in future we would never be free from the awful threat of nuclear weapons. My poem would not have won a prize in the relief and euphoria of 1945 however, apart from the ironic fact that in those days poems were expected to rhyme and scan!

Victory Poem I

This is our day of victory,
The starting-day of Peace;
Through bitter years of war we toiled
To earn this glad release.
The evil things we fought are quell'd:
The justice of our cause upheld.

But some there are who will not hear
The sentiments we voice;
And many aching hearts are left
Too lonely to rejoice:
This is the price that we have paid;
The sacrifice we grimly made.

And though our task at last is done,
A greater lies ahead;
We owe it our returning sons,
We owe it to our dead:
A World secure from want and pain,
Where peace and freedom firmly reign.

And so, amid the joyous sounds
Of this triumphant day,
We kneel to Him who blessed our cause,
With grateful hearts, to pray;
And, as the battle echoes cease,
We dedicate our lives to peace.

23rd April 1945

Victory Poem II

The bells are ringing joyously;
And merrily on high
From ev'ry building, ev'ry home,
The flags of victory fly.
The people gaily celebrate
And well deserve the right,
For this has been a people's war:
Their will to urge the fight
Has forced the enemy to yield
The final stricken battlefield.

The task was weary, grim and long,
But now that it is done,
No longer are we forced to bear
The evil of the Hun;
No further need for splendid youths,
But tasting life, to die;
No fear of death, unheralded,
From bright and cheerful sky;
No fear that those for whom we yearn
In distant lands, may not return.

But now we face, if all our work
Is not to prove in vain,
A greater task; to see that war
Can never rise again;
To build a finer, sweeter World,
A future bright and clear;
That all may earn an honest wage,
Secure from want and fear.
With grateful hearts we kneel and pray
For peace, enduring from this day.

27th April 1945

Victory

by G.I.Lee

The battle's won. Across the weary earth
The many nations that men thought had died,
Defenceless, meek, ignobly crucified,
Have proved the Resurrection. Not with mirth
And empty laughter do we bid the war
Farewell, but rather, quietly, in a deep
Proud grief and heartfelt gratitude we'll weep
For those there was no time to mourn before.
Then, taking up the challenge that they willed
As legacy - the work they would have done -
With fresh foundations we will start to build
The world anew, confident, fearing none,
Nor resting till the pledge has been fulfilled
Beyond their dreams. The battle's just begun!

April 1945

Audrey

(Written for Lieut. Stan Rumble: Canadian Army)

I could not love my Lady more,
And when we are apart
I sometimes wonder how I live,
Since Audrey has my heart.

Her disposition's sweet and kind,
And cheerful as the sun;
She smiles, and all the world is bright:
To be with her is fun.

Soft dimples play around her lips,
Her eyes are friendly brown:
Her figure irresistible:
Her hair a raven crown.

I daily thank the Providence
That gave me such a wife:
If she should die, I could not live,
For Audrey is my life.

10th May 1945

The Parting

(To Nora Mackney)

Although we tried so often to pretend
That you and I would never have to part;
With plans for future days that we could spend;
The truth was ever saddening the heart.

The moment came that we had come to dread,
With promises to "Always keep in touch;"
The things we'd planned to say were left unsaid
For platitudes; and yet they meant as much.

Not far from tears, who vowed to be so brave;
In close embrace, and hungrily, we kiss'd;
And then you ran: beneath the lamp to wave,
Before you vanished in the darkened mist.

I longed to call you back to my embrace,
With yearning such as I had never known,
And yet a second parting dare not face;
And so I turned, and walked away, alone.

22nd August 1945

I dedicated this poem to Nurse Nora Mackney, who had agreed to marry me until she learned that her existing fiancé, a Lieutenant in the Welsh Regiment who had been reported 'missing believed killed', was actually a prisoner-of-war and seriously disabled, and she could not break her promise to him or ignore what she believed now to be her duty to care for him.

Finis

The end has come: the last faint sigh of breath
Has left the shrunken frame that once had throbbed
With eager life. The long and tortured hours
While hope that faltered, rose, then fell again,
Exhausted it with battle, and at length
Betrayed the stubborn last-remaining strength.

What of the spirit: is that also dead,
Or does it from some higher plane exult
In freedom won at last; and linger yet
To see the tragic, wasted body here;
The weary limbs, the tired and careworn face,
Laid deep within their final resting-place ?

We do not know: nor can we ascertain
Until these virile forms we pride in now,
Shall take that same dread path of gaining-age:
That path of slow decay and failing pow'rs:
Until they yield their small remaining worth
To that triumphant, coldly-waiting earth.

13th January 1946

London Fog

Here in the street the traffic sounds are hushed
To mourn the light of day that never came;
Or fog, like cotton-wool, has dulled the ears.
The roadside lamps are pow'rless to assist
Faint eyes of cars, that feel a cautious way;
And cannot pierce the gloom, whence shadow-forms
Emerge, collide, apologize, move on
About their hidden ways beyond the mist.

And in the park the silence is of death;
Perhaps the still-born day is buried here
Among the trees, where naked branches reach
To find the air above the choking fog:
Gaunt and twisted limbs that grope in space
Like frenzied hands, that clutch above the grave
That draws a lost and helpless wanderer
To strangled rest, in some enfolding bog.

The vilely crawling monster hugs the ground,
Invades the mouth and fouls the stifled lungs;
To window climbs, in wraiths of smoking dirt,
As though to seek fresh, unbenighted prey:
And underneath this all-embracing shroud
Of yellow filth: this unexpected night:
A blinded city gropes a helpless way,
And pitifully cries in vain for light.

21st January 1946

Unoriginal Reflections In A Library

Beside those heavy-burdened shelves
I thought, how there was stored
The knowledge of the Universe:
A vast and priceless hoard
Of all the wisest men had said,
Or thought, since time began:
The hard-collected wisdom
And experience of Man.

I reasoned then; of all those books
Whose covers mocked at me,
Although I lived a splendid age,
A fraction would I see:
And humbly thought, though I had read
And studied not a few,
How much there still remained to learn:
How little yet I knew.

1st February 1946

The End Of The Affair

Was it love or loneliness
That made you favour me
With vows of true affection ? I agree
That much of common interest
And mutual thought was there,
And many things we both enjoyed;
And there were moments rare,
Which time could not improve,
When passion governed unrestrained:
But was there ever love ?

For now, while I have been away,
The solace that you sought
Was found elsewhere. It's all too plain
That now your foremost thought
Is not of me. Your interests
And friends have changed a deal:
That you would rather be with them
You cannot well conceal;
Nor does the fact distress.
It's over now: you called it love,
But was it loneliness ?

17th February 1946

Armageddon

The century we know was young, unschooled,
When first the blood of guiltless youth was shed
In payment for mistakes by those who ruled:
And this was war to end all war, they said.

A score of years had scurried by since then
When conflict, worse than any in the past,
Had further shamed the histories of men:
And once again we said, "This was the last."

But ever more among the nations, greed,
Distrust and bitter jealousy are rife;
From whence t'is but a minor step indeed
To armoured strength and universal strife.

And though my pray'rs could not be more sincere
For lasting peace, and not mere breathing-space;
The only war to end all wars, I fear,
Will be the one that ends the human race.

23rd February 1946

Outdoor Girl

I know you nurse a yearning,
Which you never can assuage
With the artificial pleasures
Of the restless modern age;
And so we board a motor-bus
And venture out of town,
And though you scarcely say a word,
I neither sulk nor frown.

Your pleasure is so obvious,
You hardly need confide
That your heart is quietly singing
To the smiling countryside;
And so my greatest wish for you
Is not of fame or pelf,
But a cosy little farmstead;
Which I know you'd wish yourself.

And there you'll have a cow or two,
Some chickens and, of course,
A stables, (since I know full well
You can't resist a horse).
And there you'll dwell in sweet content
And never ask for more;
While the lowliest of beggars
Would be welcome at your door.

But you've no time for happiness
You cannot freely share;
And so I make another wish:
That I may join you there.

2nd March 1946

Eternal Truth

I wearied of the fellowship of men
That fed the nagging care within my breast,
And walked the barren hills in search of peace:
To reach the sea unsated in my quest.
Here ragged promontories tapered forth
Like granite roots uncovered by the tide;
Or horny fingers, clutching fast the sand,
As though the pounding waves could be denied.
For long I watched the irritated seas
Wash inlets they and time had worn away,
And thought how long the waves had washed that shore,
To bite so deeply in that solid clay.
For Man has measured time in days and years,
But measured by the sea: the granite shelf:
A thousand human spans were scarce of note;
As little consequence as Man himself.
I thought, if I am then so very small
This robe of care, which I am apt to don,
Is wasted time: I'll throw it to the waves
That here will sigh long after I am gone.
My fate is cast: what use is it to pray ?
For He who rules this vast eternity,
Of which I form so mere a particle,
Can have no kindly interest in me.
My soul replied, "Because His realm is vast
God hath both time and space to know of all,
And nothing is forgotten in his World,
Unworthy though it seem: however small.
Man cannot sanely live, unless with hope
Of life beyond our brief chaotic day:
Of purpose in his short existence here:
His faith in God: and Man will always pray.

31st May 1946

Camaraderie

Out of the hate of war; the ghastly conflict;
From tortured hearts that still refuse to yield;
A single boon arises, noble, splendid;
And in and out of battle stays reveal'd.
A friendship born of mutual fear and danger,
Remaining true until the dying breath;
Forged 'mid the roar of guns, the smoke of battle,
And sealed with pain, amid the smell of death.

That comradeship remains when war is ended,
And ever shall while men survive to tell;
To raise a smile with some inspired reminder;
A hush for some remembered friend who fell:
A comradeship of men who dared together
A greater hell than even Satan delves:
Who offered all they had, and asked for nothing,
And found their best reward among themselves.

8th November 1946

Old-Fashioned Christmas

Christmas, I love.
More years have passed than I would care to state,
Since I would hang, above my bedroom grate,
The biggest stocking I could beg or trace,
And hope the gifts might fill a pillow-case;
And I have long-since joined the ranks who say
Unselfishly, "I'd heed not Christmas Day
If only for myself, but I <u>must</u> make
A special effort, for the children's sake."
I now confess, the same delightful thrill
Enfolds me each December, as it will
I hope, as long as life in me remains.
I love it all: the splendid model trains
So busily at work in toy bazaars,
('See Santa Claus, and take a trip to Mars'):
The decorated shops, the crowds each day;
The planning that so often goes astray;
The wrappings, strings and paper piled awry;
The scribbled list of names and things to buy,
(A calendar will do for Auntie Kate:
I really <u>mustn't</u> leave the cards too late).
I love the kitchen-help, that starts away
The recipe evolved in Grandma's day;
The stoning, peeling, mincing that occurs
Before the three official lucky stirs.
And then the carols: first the noises-off,
The faulty start, the giggles and the cough
Before, with varied keys but hopeful hearts,
At last the tale of Good King Wenc'las starts,
(But never ends), before that knock so terse:
I wonder, do they know the second verse ?
These simple joys that somehow never pall:
I love them all.

Then Christmas Eve:
The kitchen, barred to greedy hands and eyes,
Whence tasty smells of early cooking rise:
The glad goodwill that charms the shopping crush
Of folk with awkward parcels, and the rush
To buy a gift, then guiltily to send
To some forgotten, unforgetful friend:
The fun of decorating; mistletoe,
And arguments on where it ought to go;
The holly-cutting, where we should not be,
And hanging trinkets on the Christmas-tree.

And then the bells, that ring a joyous peal
To call the faithful ones to church, to kneel:
"O come adore Him," sing the bells of home,
"Venite Adoremus," bells of Rome;
The message is the same, however styl'd;
A fellowship around the Holy Child ....

Then walking home, through streets grown quiet and still
Except for laughter, borne on the midnight chill,
From cheerful little groups that homeward go
With crunching feet, in yet untrodden snow.

Then Christmas Day:
The bells that ring, "A Saviour is born ..... "
And "Merry Christmas" shouts that greet the morn
When even sluggards dare not linger late,
With gifts to set beside each breakfast plate:
Parcels wrapped in ways that might deceive
Observant, X-ray eyes on Christmas Eve:
(There's breakfast too, but no one pays it heed).
The exclamations, "Just the thing I need !"
As wrappings are explored with grateful cries,
And little acts of well~assumed surprise;
"Well, there's a kindly thought, a pipe no less:
Exactly what I want, how did you guess ?"
Then comes the stroll, by snow-encrusted way,
With garment-presents worn in proud display;
That stroll to gain a healthy appetite,
Which ends so often in a snowball-fight.

I like the cheerful bustle prior to lunch,
The table-laying, carving, and the punch
That starts the festive drinking of the day:
The quantities that each one puts away
Of turkey, tasty stuffing and, of course,
Of Christmas pudding, cloaked in brandy sauce:
The merry talk, the cracker-pulling snaps,
The mottoes and the comic paper-caps;
Until the hush that comes as luncheon ends:
A quiet toast is drunk to "Absent Friends."
Then ev'ryone is too full to aspire
To more than forty winks beside the fire,
Until the joy of draughts of tea to heal
The work of lunch, that thirst-provoking meal,
With Christmas cake in gay and proud display,
(White Eskimoes, and polar bears at play):
"It seems a shame to cut .... it looks so nice ....

Well then, perhaps, but just a <u>little</u> slice ..."
Then after tea the table's briskly clear'd
For sundry games, amusing, noisy, weird;
The modern ones, that last a fleeting day,
And then the ones that Grandpa loved to play.
'Till supper, (turkey cold, with crisp mince pies},
And then, before this day of pleasure dies,
To gather round the fire, put out the light,
For tales of ghosts and phantoms at midnight;
(Though ev'ry tale is somewhat humour-clad);
And finally to bed, a little sad.

Why sad, you ask ?
Perhaps because the friendliness and cheer
May not outlive the old and trusted year:
The dear, familiar year so nearly through,
With faint distrust at heart of something new.
Perhaps because the ties of home and friends,
So strong today, relapse when Christmas ends;
And kinsfolk, homeward drawn for Christmas Day,
Will soon be once again upon their way.
Perhaps because the world neglects the ties
Of Bethlehem where, in a manger, lies
The Little Child around whose radiance bright
All Christian men in brotherhood unite
At Christmastide, when hope seems fruitful still
Of peace on Earth, to men of true goodwill.

December 1946

Aftermath

What has war done to the Youth of the World?
It has trained him; mentally to be alert always, and to think swiftly;
Physically to endure, when ev'ry nerve and muscle pleads for rest:
To endure without food, without sleep, and often without hope.
It has taught him to gaze on the friend who fell beside him in battle,
With less compassion and anger than inward relief:
Relief that the bullet found a heart other than his own;
But relief followed instantly by guilt that will never go away.
It has taught him to think of the enemy framed in the sights of his rifle
Without pity, but with only the kill-or-be-killed instincts of the jungle;
And not as a man like himself, with an anxious wife and children;
With a small house, and a garden in which to rest on Summer ev'nings:
As a man who cares as little for the purpose of the war as he does himself,
And is even now thinking longingly of home ....

War has made him incurably restless, in a world grown madly impatient;
It has caused him to seek any form of gaudy entertainment promising
forgetfulness.
It has shown him there is nothing so mean, so lacking-in-glory as war;
And the common peoples of the earth desire only friendship and peace;
But there always will be war, because their Rulers and Mentors lead them away
from peace.
It has taught him that the common peoples must unite and destroy the causes
of war
Before their Rulers fail again, and they perish with the whole of the species of
Humankind

15th February 1947

Inquest

"The balance of his mind disturbed,"
The Law was heard to say;
But others, who were not so kind,
"He took the coward's way."
I did not argue, though I knew
I never could agree;
For would a coward take a step
That braved Eternity ?
At best, complete oblivion;
At worst, an unknown shore
On which, perhaps, this very act
Would damn him evermore.

I would not wish to end my life
Before the appointed day;
But I'd never have the courage
To adopt the "Coward's way."

27th January 1948

Epitaph For An Outspoken Person

Never the one to ignore offence
In case it was not design'd;
She snapped right back with a sharp retort,
For she always spoke her mind.

No time had she for little white lies,
When the truth was not so kind:
No one who loved her, loved her for long,
For she always spoke her mind.

She exposed illusions: none could rest,
To his failings haply blind:
Was the constant hub of verbal fray,
For she always spoke her mind.

No word unsaid that was best unsaid;
No 'sleeping dog' left reclin'd:
She died alone, in a friendless state,
For she always spoke her mind.

28th January 1971

The Final Questions

O how shall I remembered be
When I am gone, and hence
Shall stand revealed for what I was,
Ungilded by pretence?
Will times when I my temper lost
And sulked when I was riled
Be talked about; or how I sang:
How often laughed or smiled?
How little children blessed my life
And filled my heart with glee?
(And Jesus said, "Who loves a child
Receives and lovest me,")
And will they catalogue the times
I failed to pass the test,
Or will one entry serve for all,
"He tried to do his best"?
Will any praise my vain attempts
To think of ev'ryone,
Or only quote the many times
I ended pleasing none?
My failures and omissions, too;
A mocked-at tale to tell?
Or will my good intentions earn
"At least he meant it well"?
And will I be remembered then
For all I left undone,
Or will my few accomplishments
Be listed, one-by-one?
I know not how my life will seem
To family and friends,
When I am left as what I was
And cannot make amends.
Just grant me one redeeming grace,
The rest judge how you may;
I loved you all, with all my heart,
Far more than words could say.

19th July 1971

Inwards And Outwards

Though Burns, in verse, implored the Pow'rs that be
To let us see the selves that others see;
I think Almighty God would be too kind
To show ourselves in truth as others find:
Without a self-deceiving veil, to see
How selfish and self-centred we can be:
How ready to condemn, assume the worst,
Or take offence. Each grudge is fully nurs'd
Although such bitterness, if not confin'd,
Will taint our lives: destroy our peace of mind.
How swiftly and impatiently we chide
Another's faults that in ourselves we hide,
(The thoughtless errors ev'ry human makes),
And readily excuse our own mistakes.
Our own misdeeds we willingly forgive
The reason being, whatever lies we live,
We know ourselves for what we strive to be,
Our fellows just by what we hear and see:
Their thoughts and failings thoughtlessly decried,
Not knowing how well-meant: how hard they tried.
That boon we ask in pray'r ought not to be
The gift to see ourselves as others see,
For that might prove a truth too sharp to face;
But rather should we beg the saving grace
To grant to those who wrong us, or offend,
That same forgiveness we ourselves extend
To all our own misdeeds: their failings shown
The tolerance we show towards our own.

24th October 1981

Extremes

Heaven is to wake, of sounds aware
From singing birds, from farms and murmuring bees;
Through opened windows breathe fresh, scented air;
And gaze on fields, and hills, and flow'rs and trees.
Hell is this: to yearn for rural joys,
But live 'mid views of brick and concrete piles:
To waken to the mounting traffic noise;
And walk the city's air-polluted miles.

Heaven is to hear great music soar,
Or listen to a rarely gifted voice,
And inwardly to sing the well-loved score,
And feel the heart exult: the soul rejoice.
Hell is this: with all one's being to long
To make those sounds that surely Heaven sent;
But not to have the voice to sing the song,
And lack the skill to play the instrument.

Heaven is a mother's selfless care;
Of wakened love to know the tender pain;
The instant gasp at beauty made aware;
The loving trust that children's hearts contain.
Hell is this: the urge to share and stress
These moments close to God; but not to find
The words and phrases aptly to express
Emotions, thoughts, that fill the heart and mind.

9th April 1982

Resolution

I think of all the tasks undone,
And burn with shame and sorrow;
I vow to do them, one by one:
I'll make a start, tomorrow.

Today I'll rest and build my strength,
'Till fit and lion-hearted;
Today I'll plan each job at length,
To make short work, when started.

I'll not await the final chime,
With no time left to borrow;
I'll labour while I still have time,
(Procrastination's such a crime),
And start right in, tomorrow.

25th May 1982

Quality of Life

How sweet and how desirable is life
Despite the sometime worry and the strain;
The beauty, and the joy, and selfless love
Can far outweigh the sadness and the pain.
If only all our faculties could stay
Alert and active 'till the final day.

How sad it is that brains that once were live
With wit: ideas: opinions widely sought;
Should atrophy with age, and be at last
Incapable of all coherent thought:
Though once respected; heard with eager ears:
Now humoured like a child of tender years.

How sad that humans should, in closing years.
As hearing dull becomes and eyesight dims,
Humiliated be by spoon-fed slops,
And lost control of functions; senses; limbs:
To end, as was in babyhood more apt,
Being changed, and cleaned, and like an infant wrapp'd.

I fear not death, but only fear to live
To be a trial to those for whom I care;
Until their love for what I was, is drowned
In pity and distaste they then may bear.
Lord, when my time comes, let me pass away
Respected, and with dignity, I pray.

10th August 1982

All And Nothing

'Tis truly said, a Jack of all the trades
Will never master be of even one:
I add that he who seeks to please all men
Is surely bound to end by pleasing none.

The man who always tries to do too much,
(Not only for himself but others too),
And tackles ev'ry task that comes his way,
Will rarely finish what he starts to do.

And he who seeks to read and expert be
On ev'ry subject underneath the sun;
May knowing be, and versed in this and that,
But never an authority on one.

At least I speak with expertise on this;
I am myself an all-and-nothing man:
The penalty is harsh and fixed for life;
The gap between success and "Also-ran."

However ....

The single-minded specialist may end with wealth and fame,
Deservedly, when all is said and done;
But the not-so-gifted dabbler with an ever-changing aim
At least has more variety and fun.

13th August 1982

A Letter On Mothering Sunday

My dear Mother:

with all my heart I yearn to let you know how very much you mean to me,
But how can I find words which will fully express my feelings:
Words which will not appear mawkish and fulsome when read or said,
But will sound as sincere as when they left my heart:
Words that are heavy enough with praise to give you pleasure and yet,
Because of that self—deprecating modesty which is so typical of you,
Will not cause you embarrassment ?

I love you
because of your zest for life, today as always, because although the
years may have slowed your limbs they have quickened your brain:
because of your interest in all around you, and in the lives and doings
of your children, your grandchildren, and your great grandchildren:
Because of your willingness to accept new ideas; your obvious enjoyment
of the simple things that give you pleasure, usually because they are
things which are also giving pleasure to others; and your readiness to
laugh at the things, so many things, that amuse you; and your laughter
is never unkind.

I love you
because of your quick and complete sympathy when any of us is in the
least trouble, or vexed with life, or suffering from some ailment of
however minor a nature; while at the same time you accept your own real
suffering without complaint and with a shrug of dismissal. Because you
never do complain, but only display irritation and impatience with yourself that the advancing years prevent you from maintaining your past level
of activities and work rate, both of which were even then greater than
most people would attempt in the full flush of vigorous youth:
because I know that when asked how you are, if you say that you are fine,
it really only means that you have had a better day than usual; and when
you reply that you are not too bad, it means that you have had a bad day;
and on the rare occasions when you reluctantly reply, "Well, not too good
really," it means that your suffering has been such that would have had
many of us moaning in bed and seeking constant attention; and I know that
you only mention it at all because you feel that you should let me know,
but even then your main concern is not to worry me unduly.

I love you
because I know that you recognize my many faults better than anyone else,
but you love me nevertheless; and that if anyone should attack me, even if
it is because of those same faults, you will defend me more strongly than
anyone else ever will:
because you sense and understand the times when I need praise and
encouragement and will give me both in full measure, when others deny me
and hurt me because of their lack of sensitivity. You pretend not to
notice my own vain pleasure in my petty accomplishments, and your kindness
of heart prevents you from saying anything that might deflate my ego.

I love you
because I know that I can come to you and tell you my secrets without any
fear that you will repeat them to others:
because I can speak to you of my failures and fears and disappointments
in the certain knowledge that you will sympathize and advise without
being cruelly critical or condemnatory:
because I can tell you of the private yearnings of my heart, my hopes and
dreams and ambitions, without any fear that you will laugh or belittle
them; because, in other words, you provide all the qualities one would
hope to find in a friend but so few friends in fact provide, because
friendships of this nature are rare indeed.

I love you
for what you are, and for all these things that make you what you are,
and because the simple truth is that you are my truest friend, as well as
my dear, my so-very-dear, Mother.

29th July 1983

Thoughts In November

The leaves of Autumn rot beneath the tree;
The shortened days dissolve in mist and gloom;
The warmth of Summer fades in memory,
And Winter's bitter days before me loom
Until I see the Spring.

The seasons of the year speed swifter by
As I approach the winter of my life,
And less can I avoid, though harder try,
The nagging question, painful as a knife,
O shall I see the Spring ?

But surely as I know, when Winter's past,
The season comes of green and tender birth;
My resurrection too, will come at last;
And in that other world, if not on Earth,
I know I'll see the Spring.

18th March 1984

True Values

I sometimes pause and think my lifetime over,
Of all I hoped and planned but failed to do:
Of wasted hours I never will recover;
Of wealth and fame I never will accrue.
I think of work that gained no recognition;
Of poems no one else has brought to tongue;
How songs matured, but never reached fruition;
Of words and music only I have sung.
It well may be, if judged by those above me,
That 'Failure' is the label they would cast;
I hope and pray that those who really love me
Will give a kinder verdict at the last.

The level that a man ambition pitches
Should be the only yardstick to compare;
For can a man, who never aimed at riches,
Be said to fail if not a millionaire ?
A man's success is all too often measured
In terms of wealth and pow'r he may possess,
Although the ones he should have loved and treasured
Have known neglect, and no true happiness.
I gave to those held dear, in youth and after,
My love and time and did not rue the cost;
And I have heard my children's happy laughter:
Worth more by far than anything I lost.

22nd May 1984

The Effort And The Achievement

McGonagall and Wordsworth were, as poets, far apart:
The one revered, whose poetry could penetrate the heart;
The other scorned and ridiculed: his poetry so bad,
To be performed in public, as a mirth-provoking fad.
But this they had in common, whether fêted or decried;
The urge to write was paramount and could not be denied.
For if it meets obscurity, or if it leads to fame,
The soul still craves expression and the effort is the same;
And though he may have inward doubts, and think it all in vain
If no one wants to print his work, or hear it read again;
He cannot judge it honestly, with bias set aside:
No father can assess his child, when blind with love and pride.
So if what I have written, be it melody or rhyme,
Was so much fruitless effort and a shameful waste of time
Remember, and please judge me with what kindness you possess,
I should have done much better but I could have done no less.

9th June 1984

Three Days

Lost yesterday I made mistakes;
I meant so well, and yet
I said and did a lot of things
I wish I could forget;
I wasted opportunities
And chances, Heaven sent;
I squandered hours of precious time
And wondered where it went.
But yesterday is history;
It's far too late to rue
The tragedy and mystery
Of all I failed to do.

Tomorrow and the future days
May tell another tale;
Perhaps I may achieve success,
Perhaps again may fail.
I'll waste no time on golden dreams,
Nor fear what may befall;
Tomorrow is too far away:
It may not come at all.

I have today to make amends
For what has gone before:
I have today to work and plan
For what may be in store.
No sentence changed, no word erased,
Will yesterday allow;
Tomorrow is an unread book:
Today is here and now.

16th April 1985

Problems

There are clever crossword puzzles
For the buffs who words befriend
And there is, if they can find it,
A solution at the end;
And mathematics experts
Know perplexities involved
With figures and with formulae
Can finally be solved.

The poet tries to set his thoughts
In metre and in rhyme;
The ultimate in puzzles;
The hypothesis sublime.
He seeks a formal pattern
For the ideas he begets,
But there may not be an answer
To the problems that he sets.

17th April 1985

Sleeping Time

When life seemed long and had no end,
And I was young and in my prime,
When finally I went to bed,
I dallied far too long a time.

But life is short, and shorter grows
With each relentless hourly chime;
And now, to spend a third asleep
Is just a waste of dwindling time.

I know that I must rest at night
Or I shall never feel my prime;
But there's so much I'd rather do
Than sleep, and waste that precious time.

6th June 1985

Pace Or Perfection

Though any job worth doing,
Is a job worth doing well;
We sadly learn that time restricts
Intentions to excel,

Should quality of workmanship
Be sacrificed to speed;
Or quality command the time
To fill the craftsman's need ?

Though most accept the slip-shod work
That time-lack justifies;
The one whose heart believes in best
Can never compromise.

And so we have this paradox,
To anger and appal;
Because the job's worth doing well,
It's never done at all.

22nd September 1985

Artistic Judgement

The urge to do creative work must be assuaged always,
No matter how the end result turns out;
Just now and then it may evoke a modicum of praise
But, oft as not, uncertainty and doubt.

One hopes to hear some words of praise, but only if sincere;
Afraid as well that others may deride
And, all too often, have to bear that sense we come to fear
Of loss and disappointment, deep inside.

For only those with prejuduce will utterly reject,
Or those pre-partial give unstinted praise;
A lukewarm view or none at all is normal to expect
Or worse, "Quite good," (that patronizing phrase).

And then the mind, 'mid strong self-doubts that have it on the rack,
Must ponder too the bigger question left;
Did those who failed to praise it, true appreciation lack,
Or was the work of quality bereft?

8th January 1986

Thought And Action

Whoever wrote the proverbs that are quoted all our days,
Themselves demeaned their value when they wanted it both ways
For, "Nothing ventured, nothing gained," is one that shapes our ends
But, "Look before you leap," is what another recommends.
An element of caut1on's more advisable than none,
But a venture never started is a project never done.
A journey of a thousand miles, the Chinese aptly say,
May loom ahead, but starts with just one step upon the way;
And anyone will vouch, who ever gazed into the deep,
The longer looked and thought about, the worse becomes the leap.
Success demands an effort; ev'ry pleasure has a price:
You cannot have a chance to win unless you throw the dice.
The Princess in the fairy-tale was often seen to wince,
You have to kiss a lot of frogs before you find a prince;
And those who struck it rich at last, in gold-rush days of old,
Dug tons of earth, and rock, and sand before they found the gold.

29th February 1988

Buried Treasure

(On reading that at any one time the bulk of the treasures of ancient
Egypt are stored in crates in the basement of the British Museum)

The treasures of the Pharoahs
'Neath the pyramids were stored,
In buried caverns, hid from human eyes;
But Carter and Carnarvon
Dug to find that priceless hoard,
And show the world their jewelled and golden prize.

The treasures of the Pharoahs
In museums now are stored,
And some are seen in popular displays;
But most, that once enriched the tombs,
Again a buried hoard;
Fill musty basements, hid from human gaze.

9th March 1988

Note To A Critic

I ask not less than honesty,
Or that you should be kind;
Remember just that here you read
The product of one mind.

The thoughts might come to someone else,
But what he chose to say
Would be composed with other words;
Arranged some other way.

I only ask you bear in mind,
When writing your critique;
It may be utter rubbish,
But at least it is unique.

13th April 1988

Human (Un)kind

Some call a man "coloured"; his true worth they slight,
While despising the hue of his skin;
But all men are coloured, from black down to white,
And their character comes from within.
Some hear no good spoken of this or that Race:
Close their minds, just like shutting a door;
And some mock the crippled; the witless debase;
While others look down on the poor.
The numerous languages keep us in bounds,
Which is often a matter of shame;
But love, as a word, may have hundreds of sounds,
Yet its meaning is always the same.
And we all have the love of our Father, above,
Though we differ in body and mind:
We are all of us joined by His kinship of love
That embraces the whole human kind.
Though divided by Race, class, or colour or creed;
Or just non-conformist or odd;
We are all of us brothers and sisters indeed:
We are all of us children of God.

26th October 1988

Cost and Compensation

A sunset brings beauty to finish the day,
But there must have been clouds in the sky;
There's joy and there's hope in a fresh start to life,
But the journey must first go awry.

The sun brings us fragrant and fresh-growing flow'rs,
But there has to be plenty of rain;
An end to long-illness brings blesséd relief,
But at first one must suffer the pain.

The joy of returning to home and to kin,
That can make such a heart-warming day,
Can only be known if the heart was first pierced
By the sorrow of going away.

26th February 1989

Positive View

The Chinese have a saying, "I complained I had no shoes,
'Till the day I met a man who had no feet,"
And few complaints or maladies are utterly bereft
Of all the things that make existence sweet.
Disasters, man or nature-caused, are tempered in distress
By deeds of sacrifice, and actions brave:
The problems and the trials of life are never quite so bad
For those prepared to face them out, and slave.
But some are ever claiming that they can't do this or that
And beaten are, before the job's begun;
While others, no more able, will confront each daunting task
And do it, for they know it must be done.
And always there are people who bemoan each trifling pain,
And suffer more by dwelling on complaints;
But others scorn the inward view: make light of ills far worse,
And sometimes even emulate the Saints.
So come to me you cheerful souls who minimise your ills,
And let us count our blessings, day-by-day;
But we've no time for pettifogging niggles and complaints:
You moaners and you groaners, stay away !

8th August 1989

94

On Growing Old

Though not so young as once I was,
(My youth seems far away),
Look back just four and twenty hours:
I've only aged a day.
I'll never be so young again,
But why give way to sorrow ?
Though young as now I'll never be,
I'm younger than tomorrow.

Too late to change , or try to hide
My faults, that may appal;
I am what time and fate have made,
Ungilded, warts and all.
No time to brood on past mistakes
I cannot now remove;
Too little now is left, to waste:
So much I still must prove.

If marked in years, the time that's left
May not hold many more;
In days, each year that's still to come
Has close to twenty score.
I'll think in days and not in years,
Each dawn with thanks I'll pray;
I know tomorrow may not come:
I'll fully live today.

12th November 1989

Grateful Prayer

There are many in the World who have not heard
The song of waking birds at break of day;
Or music played; or heard the spoken word;
Or laughter of a little child at play.
How petty then, my own complaints appear;
I thank you humbly, Lord, that I can hear.

There are many in the World who have not seen
The colours of the flow'rs, or fields, or trees;
Or face of loved one, smiling, sad, serene;
Or sunsets, heathered mountains, restless seas.
Ignore my vain complaints, and pardon me;
I thank you humbly, Lord, that I can see.

There are many in the World who live confin'd
To prison-chair, or close-embracing bed;
Whose limbs will not obey the urging mind;
Undignified: are washed, and dressed, and fed.
Forgive my small complaints as foolish talk;
I thank you, Lord, that I can move and walk.

There are many in the world who live alone
With none to love, communicate, or care;
No joy of hugging child that I have known;
No fond caress from one with love to spare.
For love of friends and kin, but these above,
I thank you, Lord, for Your redeeming love.

27th March 1990

Test Of Faith

June 18th 1991

Through all my life, until this worst of days,
I turned to you when Fate was less than kind;
You gave me solace, faith renewed, and praise
While, kindly, to my failings seeming blind;
And now your selfless life has reached its end
I've lost, not just my Mother, but my friend.

I anguished as you lay in restless pain
And, if I could, I would not beg you stay,
Though yearning for your lucid voice again,
To live another tortured, weary day.
And now, in pain-free joy, at peace you dwell
In God's fair Kingdom you deserved so well.

I know, in time, that I shall join you there,
For so have I believed, and so was taught
But, rising from my sorrow and despair,
I question: is it just a wishful thought ?
Lord, help me now to hold what I believe,
And shun the doubts that haunt me as I grieve.

30th January 1992
(Her birthday)

Immortality

" .... I might perhaps leave something so written
to aftertimes, as they should not willingly let it die."

John Milton

John Milton, modest, though sublime
His talents, wrote to satisfy
His wish that those in aftertime
Not willingly should let it die.
The all that I and Milton share,
(If only it were more!), is aim,
But he had worth beyond compare,
While I shall never bask in fame
Or, likely, even near the verge
My talents, gained or handed down,
Being less than my creative urge:
Too few to generate renown.
But recognition yet may lie
In someone further down the line,
Whose genes renew and fortify
The meagre talents that were mine.
Perhaps some generation new,
The next, or next but two or three,
Will write the words, and music too,
Of songs that live in memory;
Or hang his pictures in the Tate;
Or sing or play at some far Prom.;
And ev'ryone will speculate,
"I wonder who he gets it from?"

14th May 1992

(Or it might equally well be 'She,' but there was no room in the line for both
pronouns. This would be just the right occasion for the use of the word
'hesh,' as suggested in the poem "Simpler Grammar" ....

Simpler Grammar

In our splendid English language, it has always seemed to me
That we badly need a pronoun for the laboured 'He or She.'
I suggest a simple answer: cause the two to inter-mesh,
So the joint third person singular becomes the one word 'Hesh;'
And then, by equal treatment, that would make the single term
To replace the two in object form, the sex-embracing 'Herm'
And, as the fog of centuries of he or she-ing clears,
We get the new possessive word, pronunciation 'hiers.'
To give a brief example of these mingled words in use,
Originally worded, on the subject of abuse,
"That he, or even sometimes she," the speaker might aver,
"Could his or her good temper lose and strike at him or her;"
But spoken with the tandem words much simpler, I affirm,
That hesh might lose hiers temper and perhaps lash out at herm.

9th January 1998

Flower of Hope

I saw a pretty sight today
That filled me with delight;
A primrose, with its yellow flow'rs
Against the snow, so white.
For what could better speak of hope
And cause the heart to sing,
Than the final snow of Winter,
With the promise of the Spring?

22nd February 1994

One Taken: One Left

How harsh the mental torment,
With forgetfulness denied,
Of a soldier, when his closest friend
Is cut down by his side,
When he it might have been who fell;
And even as he grieved
To feel, while hating what he felt,
Instinctively relieved.
Succeeding years will not abate
His oft-recurrlng grief;
Still haunted by the guilt and shame
Of feeling that relief.

llth November 1994

Colours Of The Season

Spring is yellow.
Yellow marks the end of Winter's run;
Hue of primrose, hue of daffodil;
Yellow of a pale and gentle sun.

Summer is red.
Red of sunset skies at end of day;
Red of England's rose in glorious bloom;
Red of fire in sun's consuming ray.

Autumn is brown.
Brown of wheat in neatly-gathered sheaves;
Brown of cushion-flow'red chrysanthemum;
Brown of splendoured trees and fallen leaves.

Winter is white.
White of snowdrop, white of Christmas rose;
White of frost on starkly naked trees;
White on all around of fallen snows.

31st March 1995

Divine Support

Lord, when I chose to follow you,
You promised you would stay
And walk with me, and talk with me,
Each step along the way;
And so, when most I needed you,
I cannot understand
Why I could only see one set
Of footprints In the sand.
He answered me, "My precious child
Know this, I love you still:
I never have forsaken you
And leave you never will;
And when you needed me the most
But noticed in your track
A single set of footprints there,
I bore you on my back."

8th March 1997

In every place where you find the
imprint of men's feet, there am I.
(The Talmud)

What Is Dying?

The ship departs; we wave farewell,
As smaller she appears
Until, the far horizon reached,
At last she disappears.
And yet we know she still exists
Although beyond our eyes;
Her beauty not one fraction less,
Unchanged in shape and size.
To those upon the other shore
She ever larger looms
And, as we sadly say, "She's gone,"
They call out, "Here she comes!"
And those to whom we said farewell
With tears and mental pain,
When we in time that journey make
Will greet us once again.

14th February 2000

With acknowledgement to Bishop Brent

I am standing upon that foreshore. A ship at my side spreads her white sails to
the morning breeze and starts for the blue ocean. She is an object of beauty and
strength, and I stand and watch her until at length she hangs like a speck of
white cloud just where the sea and sky come down to mingle with each other.
Then someone at my side says, "There! She's gone!" Gone where? Gone from
my sight, that's all. She is just as large in mast and spar and hull as ever she
was when she left my side; just as able to bear her load of living freight to the
place of her destination. Her diminished size is in me, not her. And just at the
moment when someone at my side says, "There! She's gone!" there are other
eyes watching her coming and other voices ready to take up the glad shout,
"Here she comes!"

.... and that is dying.

Bishop Brent: 1862-1926

Contrasting Attitudes

The optimist enjoys a sunny nature,
The pessimist is fettered by dismay
And ever sees his glass as being half-empty:
But his half-full, the optimist will say.
For him to lose life's game is not considered,
The other's hopes of winning it are nil;
To optimists the worst may never happen,
The pessimist is ever sure it will,
And through his days is sunk in grim foreboding.
The optimist with hope and faith is buoy'd,
And never short of friends and good companions,
The former viewed as someone to avoid.
In practice, though, to fear the worst is better;
To look upon the bright side ill-advised;
The optimist can suffer disappointment,
The pessimist be pleasantly surprised.

3rd April 2000

Last Message

I've always been emotional and find, in later years,
That memories and sad events will have me shedding tears;
So if, when I am near my end, you notice that I cry,
It will not mean I suffer pain or that I fear to die,
But sorrow felt at leaving you: you gave such happiness;
And knowledge that my passing on will cause you much distress
For, if our feelings were so deep we found it hard to tell:
I loved you both with all my heart, and know you loved me well.
And though I may have left this life, be sure I'm with you still;
And all we've been, and all we had, again, in time, we will.

5th May 2000

Home Help

The moment when, each week, we part
Is like approaching doom,
I know the days about to start
Will largely be of gloom.
Sweet thoughts of you will wake my mind
At morning's early light,
And be the last that I shall find
Before I sleep, each night;
And interrupt my thought-linked train
Through all the hours between,
And tasks of either hand or brain
Without you, little mean;
Until the days that slowly pass'd
Have counted down from seven
And Friday dawns, to bring at last
Three hours of perfect Heaven.

8th October 2000

The Sirens In My Life

In ancient times the constant fear would loom
That sirens might lure seamen to their doom;
Now rescue sirens sound throughout the day.
In one such Godsend once myself did pray
That God would keep my little girl alive
In time for expert help, who did survive.
In boyhood, ev'ry other noise to drown,
Queen Mary's siren boomed across the town.
I ran each day to reach the workers' gate
Before the siren blew and made me late
Then worked, and watched the clock with mounting glee,
Until it blew again and set me free.
And then opposing sirens: one brought fear,
The other signalled skies again were clear;
Emerging on one dank November day
To find the home I loved was blown away.
Then later still, like mariners of old,
A siren lured me, in her arms to fold;
To give some years of happiness and gain,
But many more of misery and pain.
And now, with four score years behind, I hold
The time-bomb one acquires on growing old
And might, I wonder, as the shadows near,
A siren be the final sound I hear?

18th February 2002

Written for the Literary Review competition: Subject 'Sirens'

Without Rhyme Or Reason

Most modern so-called poetry
Is really only prose
Arranged in lines of varied lengths,
With reason, I suppose;
But though the writing may be fine,
Devoid of other skill.
The World at large knows not my name,
And likely never will
But, like the bards of former days,
For better or for worse,
I try to put my thoughts and views
In rhyming, scanning verse.
I often fail: may even be
Impossible my aim,
But sometimes I succeed and earn
A mild but local fame.
With poems like the present,
That is metrical, and rhymes,
Would greater fame have come to me
If born in former times?
Revered, and loved and quoted
Like the Poets of the Lakes,
Or laughed at, like McGonagall,
For rubbish and mistakes?

14th February 2003

It Could Be You

Some hope to win the Lottery
And think, one day, they will,
And gamble what they can't afford
To taste that weekly thrill;
And yet the chance of six in line
To win that dream of gold
Is only one in millions,
When the honest truth is told.

The same misguided optimists,
Whose chance is almost nil,
Hope not to have an accident
And think they never will;
And yet, for those who own a car
And normal journeys drive,
Their chances of an accident
Are one in nine point five.

15th July 2003

Literary Review Competition: Subject: Gambling

One-Sided Love

You cannot understand my love
Because of what you lack;
Afraid to give yourself in full
And always holding back.
My love for you is intertwined
With all I think and do:
A giving love, not merely gifts,
But physically, too.
A love that has to forward go
With neither pause nor swerve;
A love you can't appreciate:
A love you don't deserve.

30th September 2004

End Of An Affair

Though looked on by the world as long-in-tooth
He loved her with the joy and ache of youth,
And ever for her company he yearned.
For only while it suited she returned
His love in equal measure, so he thought,
But really from amusement and in sport;
For what to him was all and ev'rything,
To her was nothing but a passing fling.
An easy conquest quickly bores and tires,
And then she sought new outlets, fresh desires
And fickle, restless nature had its way.
Full knowing that she ruled his ev'ry day;
In all his life supplied the vital part;
Without the least concern she broke his heart.
Deprived of any will to stay alive
He could not all the stress and pain sunrive,
And when he reached his final place of rest
The message with her flow'rs said, "All the best!"

20th November 2004

Battle Of The Sexes

Since Eve fulfilled the serpent's plan and ate forbidden fruit,
Like rampant Casanovas, men have been in hot pursuit
Of women, with the shameful aim to have a sexual fling,
Without a true commitment to a future wedding-ring;
And countless books have aired the themes of hopeful girls betray'd:
In melodramas wicked squires seduced a village maid.
Then came the contraceptive pill, the feminists to boost:
Extremists even voiced the claim that women ruled the roost.
So now the sexes both enjoy their fill of sexual fun,
And women may have freedom gained but men, it is, who won.

21st January 2006

Written for the Literary Review Competition: Subject: The Modern Gentleman

Liquid Of Destiny

The Arabs say we're masters of the words we only think,
But slaves of what we choose to say which, if revealed in ink,
Though simple in ingredients and harmless in itself,
May judged to be a libel and may decimate our pelf.
lnk registers our date of birth and finally our death,
And rules and governs all our lives as long as we draw breath;
It penned the laws and royal assent that framed the precious charter
Of freedom and democracy enshrined in Magna Carta,
And all the countless documents that history records,
Of treaties that have led to peace or, often, crossing swords.
"This paper that I hold aloft means peace in all our time!"
Cried trusting Neville Chamberlain, in ignorance sublime,
But Hitler made his evil plans before the ink had dried,
And plunged the World in conflict, so that millions fought and died;
And ink has also put the seal on countless wedding vows
That ended in unfaithfulness and never-ending rows;
On warrants, writs and pardons that may life or death decide,
And honours and citations that are amply justified,
Though hopes and dreams are shattered, and the tears of failure shed,
Through criticism, censure and rejection when it's red;
Yet ink has put in written form the thoughts, to grace our days,
Of poets and philosophers, and Shakespeare's matchless plays.
It's hard, if not impossible, in retrospect to think
Of anything with greater pow'r than simple pen and ink.

19th February 2006

Written for 'Literary Review' Competition: Subject INK.

Never Too Humble

The birds have nests; the foxes holes
And, equally compelling,
In humans there's an inbuilt urge
To get themselves a dwelling,
Where friends may take a glass of wine
And have a good-old natter.
As people say, regarding size,
It really doesn't matter;
What good's a mansion filled with gloom
That echoes up to rafter ?
Prefer a cott, where ev'ry room
Is filled with love and laughter;
And offsprings find their feelings drawn,
However far they roam,
Like some innate magnetic force
To Mother, and the home.

17th September 2006

Written for The Literary Review: Subject "Home."

Common Factor

Other men have climbed mountains, or conquered the seas,
Or adventured as I could not do;
Flourished rich or grown famous in varied degrees,
Or committed what later would rue.
Even I, in my failures or times of success,
In my search for fultilment or fun
Though unlikely, yet possible nevertheless,
May have done what no other has done.
We are all, in our heights or to what depths we sink,
Made unique in our various ways;
In our actions, emotions and all that we think.
But the moon, through the length of our days,
Watches over us all and our varying deeds,
Like a far-distant yellow balloon;
And no matter what colours, or races or creeds,
We have all of us gazed at the moon.

8th February 2007

Written for the "Literary Review" competition: Subject "The Moon."

Home Is Where The Hearth Is

I've journeyed far, on what has been a long and varied road,
And thank my Maker gratefully for all that he bestow'd.
I've known the boon of timely help from friends who stood the test;
And loved, and laughed, and talked and sung, (and laughter was the best).
My heart has soared when orchestras performed a lifting score,
And thrilled to watch the angry waves attack a rocky shore.
I've gloried in the country scenes that soothed my town-tired eyes;
And marvelled at the rolling clouds, and dawn and sunset skies.
I've been to strange exotic Lands I thought I wished to roam,
And travelled widely round the World, but found I yearned for home;
And learnt no brief, exciting thrill of voyage on land or sea
Can match the joy of coming back to home and family,
Whose members leave to seek what fates the future may reveal
In all directions, heading forth like spokes within a wheel;
The hub of which will ever be of kith and kin and home:
A magnet that will still attract, however far they roam.

18th July 2007

Written for the Literary Review Competition: Subject: Home

Sonnet Of Poetic Truth

A proper poet seeks in metric form
To phrase his thoughts with, where required, a rhyme;
In words of syllables that fit the norm;
Which sometimes proves impossible, in time.

The modern so-called bard writes down his thoughts
Without a care for scansion or for rhymes,
Or metric form; in lines of varied sorts,
With even sentence split by verse at times.

No matter how profound his reverie,
Or beautiful or apt the words he chose,
Or how arranged or split the lines may be,
The end result can still be only prose.

How much more skill it takes to strive and plan
To write one's thoughts in words that rhyme and scan.

27th October 2007

As part of an ongoing and amicable difference of opinion, l sent the above
sonnet to my half-brother Mike Shannon, actor and poet. He replied with
another sonnet ....

Many Kinds Of Poetry - A Sonnet.

Though Shakespeare's sonnet style I much approve,
And Donne and Milton's verses celebrate,
And seek out Yeats within his Sylvan Grove,
Nor Rhyming poets seek to denigrate:

Yet I will write as freely as I need
As Auden, Larkin, Hughes and Graves have done,
I follow where these rarest spirits lead
Though further off than earth is from the sun.

If poetry is not to be confined
Forever in a rigid metric scheme,
It needs to show the treasures of the mind
In constant change of form, and style and theme.

If unrhymed verse you truly can't abide -
Yet it will thrive with rhymed verse side by side !!

Mike Shannon 28.12.07

His argument was irrefutable, but he had typed his sonnet on a battered old typewriter, badly in need of a new ribbon, so I replied with..............

Honourable Draw, Or Only Round Three?

Your arguments can never be decried,
With such renowned examples and their feats;
Though I in turn, to bolster up my side,
Refer to Wordsworth, Tennyson and Keats.

Your apt reply, rewarding equal praise
To no restraints, or form with rhyming sounds
That children learn and quote throughout their days,
Was great: my admiration knows no bounds.

But though my sonnet merits lesser hype,
I think it likely keen computer-men
Would, in their scorn for fading ancient type,
For presentation, give me ten from ten.

If poetry alone provides the test,
The laurel wreath is yours: I give you best!

3rd January 2008

Merciless Marion

I'd reached a time when my remaining years
Seemed such that I should never know again
A love that ev'ry waking thought endears,
And mingles passion with the sweetest pain.
But suddenly, all other things above,
We merged, as no one else could comprehend;
Together we explored the realms of love;
A course you glibly promised not to end.
But shallow you, and promise, proved to be
When, cleanly as a surgeon's ruthless knife,
To suit yourself, without a thought for me,
You callously incised me from your life;
My endless love with sheer contempt to spurn,
And break my heart, without the least concern.

24th November 2007

Body of Christ

Yours is the only body Christ has now;
His eyes to see, His humble head to bow;
His hands to do His work and bless each day.

Yours are the only feet on which He walks;
Yours is the only mouth through which He talks;
Yours are the knees on which He kneels to pray.

Yours is the voice He needs to spread His word;
The ears by which His Father's voice is heard;
His ears, and yours, to listen and obey.

Yours is the will He needs, the poor to feed
And seek and tend to those who comfort need;
To be His means, and follow in His way.

10th February 2008

From The Prayer of Saint Teresa of Avila:

Christ has no body now
on earth but yours,
no hands but yours
no feet but yours.
Yours are the eyes through
which Christ's compassion
is to look out to the world.
Yours are the feet by which
he is to go about doing good.
And yours are the hands by
which he is to bless us now.

Expectancy Of Life

It's said that God has given men
A life of three score years and ten,
And I know well, yet have no fears,
That I have passed that span of years
But thankful, when I ope my eyes,
No less for dull than sunny skies,
That God, to whom I daily pray,
Has given me another day.
A day when, hopefully, I win
The love of loyal friends and kin;
Another day to please the eye
With trees and flow'rs, and sea and sky;
Another day to be enjoyed,
And usefully to be employed,
And possibly new ways to find
That aid my fellow humankind;
Another day to laugh and sing
From joy that little children bring;
Another chance in hope to pray
That I may see another day.

October 8th 2008

Friendship

My friend accepts me as I am,
With all my faults well-known;
Indulges all the ego-trips
And vanity I've shown.
I know if others slander me
My friend will fight my cause,
And aid me, should I be in need,
Without a moment's pause.
Despite my failings and misdeeds,
And moments of ill-will
If life's events have angered me,
My friend will love me still.
We treat our views with full respect
If either disagrees;
We laugh together frequently
At life's absurdities.
I know my friend will weep for me
When I shall reach my end,
Which saddens me; but constantly
I thank God for my friend.

4th March 2010

Chemotherapy

The greatest artists ever known to fame
Faced blank and simple canvas at the start
Which, by their skill and genius, became
A beautiful and priceless work of art.

What Philistine, to his eternal shame,
With precepts rising from a mundane heart,
Could then allow a fussy, ornate frame
Detract attention from that glorious art?

You may well think it quite enough to bear
The knowledge of a cruel internal flaw,
And suffer illness rising from its care;
And deem the loss of hair the final straw.

But all can see, without that frame of hair,
The beauty of your face, beyond compare.

31st May 2010

The Stronger Emotion

With cruelty and ruthless in extreme,
And suddenly, you cut me from your life
While I, if factors had not ruled it out,
Would willingly have taken you for wife.
E'er since, ignored and like a leper spurned
And, not being told, I cannot fathom why
You hate me now for what I am or did,
And clearly care not if I live or die.
I wish I could erase you from my thoughts
But many things recall you to my mind;
I ought to hate you now for what you've done
But, as is wisely said, true love is blind.
A love I'd like to lose but does not die;
At best to dormant lie but oft recur:
I cannot hate you now for what you are:
I love you too much still for what you were.

18th April 2012